D1326119

FOR JEN

WITH SPECIAL THANKS TO LINDSEY, LINDA

MEG, SARAH AND COLIN

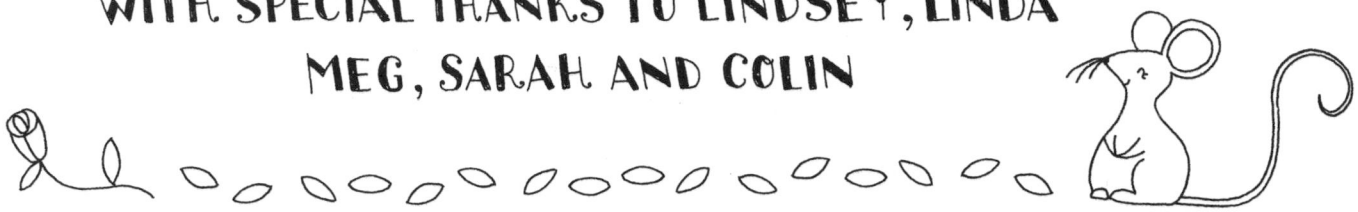

AN ART ADVENTURE

AROUND THE NATIONAL GALLERIES OF SCOTLAND

BY EILIDH MULDOON

THE NATIONAL GALLERIES OF SCOTLAND ARE FULL OF WONDERFUL THINGS TO SEE. SOMEWHERE THERE IS A STATUE OF FAMOUS SCOTTISH POET ROBERT BURNS...
...CAN YOU FIND IT?

PAY US A VISIT!

WITH THIS BOOK YOU CAN...

- USE THE MAP AT THE BACK OF THE BOOK TO PLAN YOUR ROUTE
- COLOUR IN THE PICTURES
- FILL IN THE EMPTY SPACES WITH THINGS YOU SEE
- ADD YOURSELF, YOUR FRIENDS AND FAMILY!

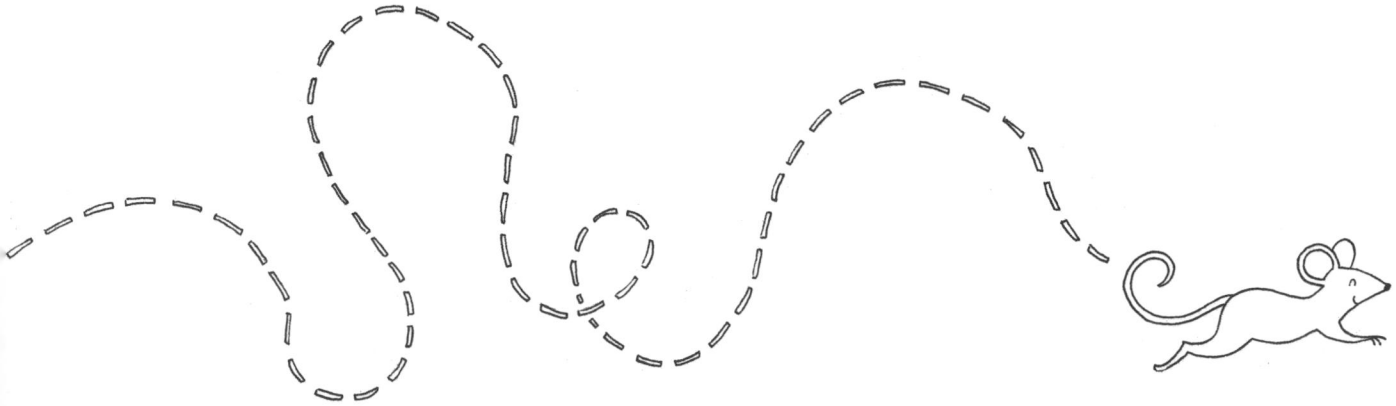

NATIONAL GALLERIES OF SCOTLAND

NATIONAL GALLERY OF SCOTLAND

RSA
TAXI

MODERN
TWO

PAOLOZ
THIS WAY U

corps
humain

MODERN ONE
GALLERIES
ART 1

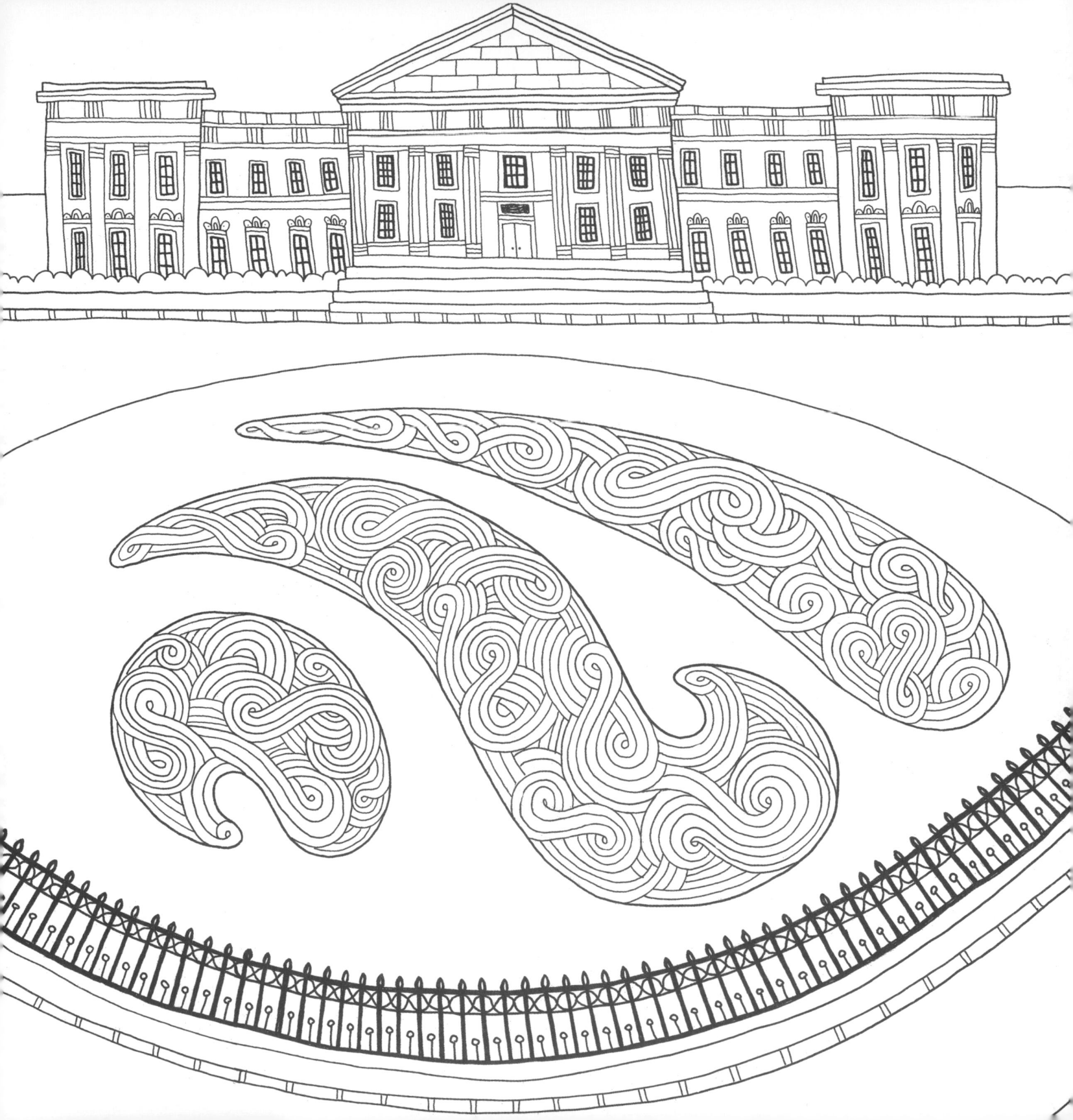

GALLERIES
ART 1

PORTRAIT
GALLERY

MODERN ONE
BELFORD ROAD
DEAN VILLAGE
DEAN BRIDGE
ZOO
MODERN TWO
WATER OF LEITH
TO THE ZOO
TO HAYMARKET TRAIN STATION
N
W
E
S
HOW DID YOU GET TO THE GALLERIES?
WALK
BUS
TRAM
CYCLE
LOTHIAN ROAD

MY ART ADVENTURE

FILL THIS SPACE WITH DOODLES

PLAN YOUR ROUTE!

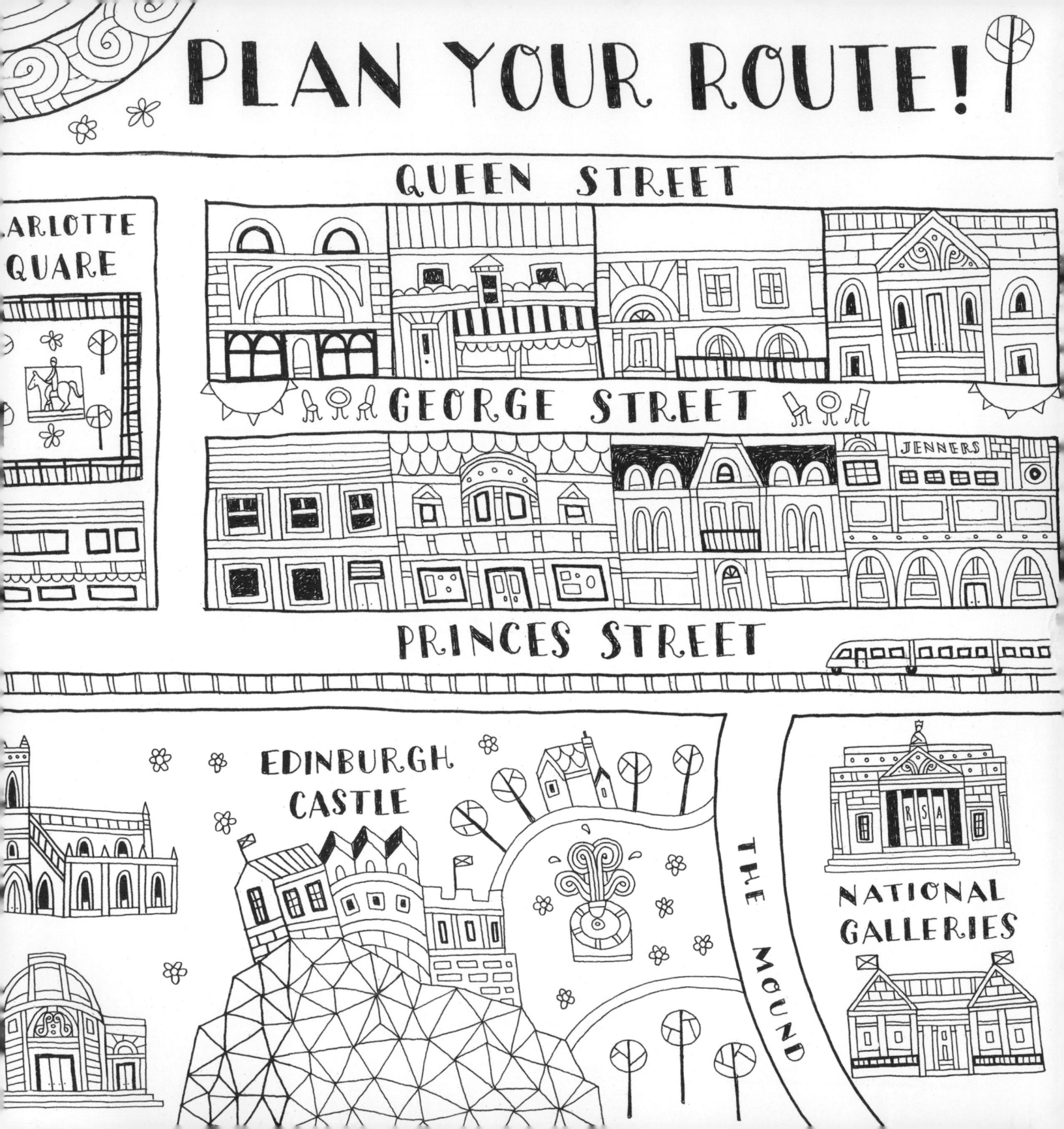

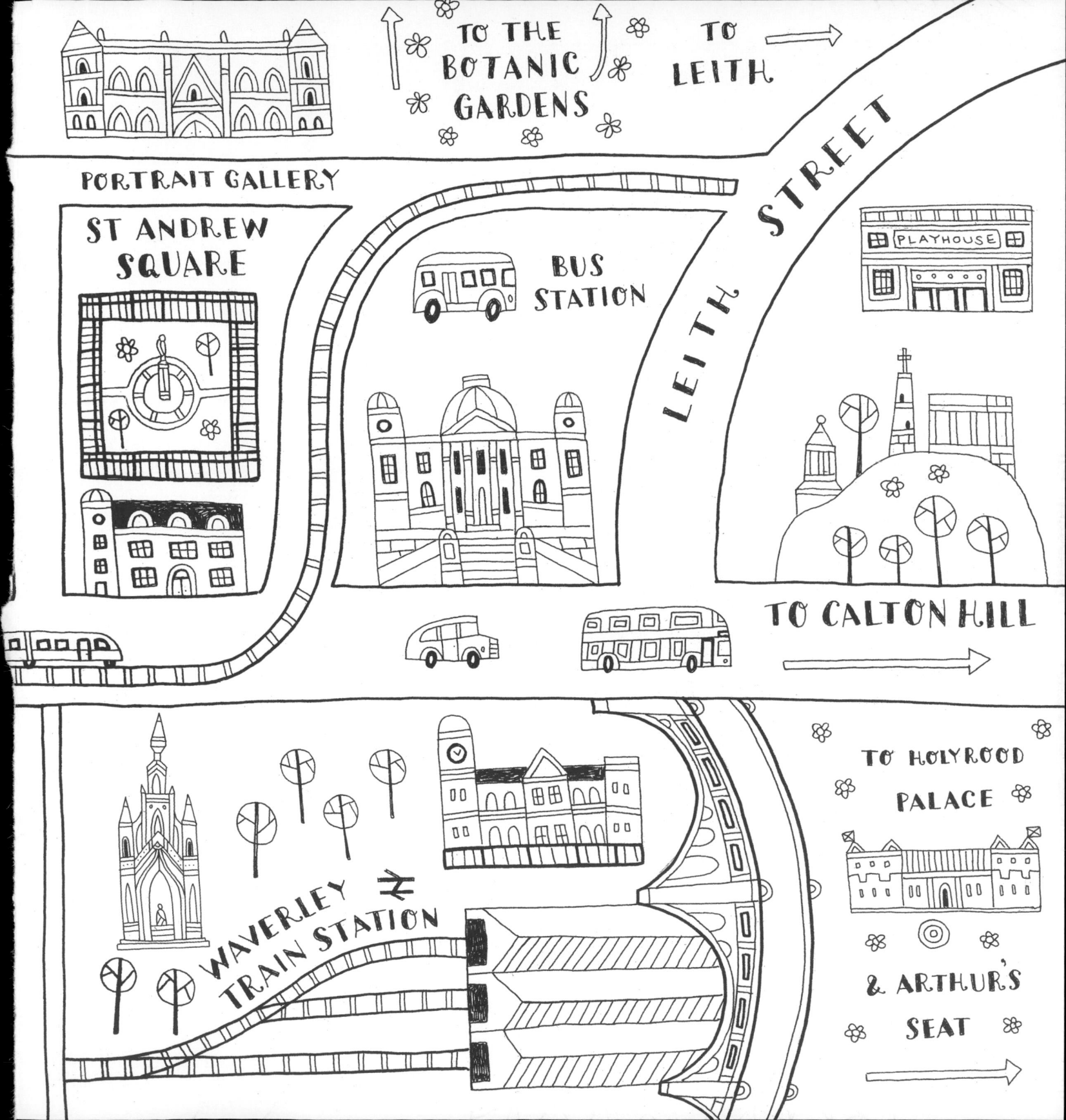
TO THE BOTANIC GARDENS
TO LEITH
PORTRAIT GALLERY
ST ANDREW SQUARE
BUS STATION
LEITH STREET
PLAYHOUSE
TO CALTON HILL
WAVERLEY TRAIN STATION
TO HOLYROOD PALACE
& ARTHUR'S SEAT

GALLERY GUIDE

NATIONAL GALLERY, THE MOUND

'THE HONOURABLE MRS GRAHAM'
BY THOMAS GAINSBOROUGH

GALLERY OF MODERN ART ONE, BELFORD ROAD

'CONVERSATIONS WITH MAGIC STONES'
BY BARBARA HEPWORTH

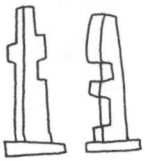

GALLERY OF MODERN ART TWO, BELFORD ROAD

'MASTER OF THE UNIVERSE'
BY EDUARDO PAOLOZZI

PORTRAIT GALLERY, QUEEN STREET

'PROCESSIONAL FRIEZE IN THE CENTRAL HALL'
BY WILLIAM HOLE

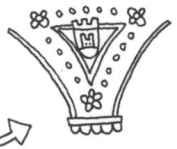

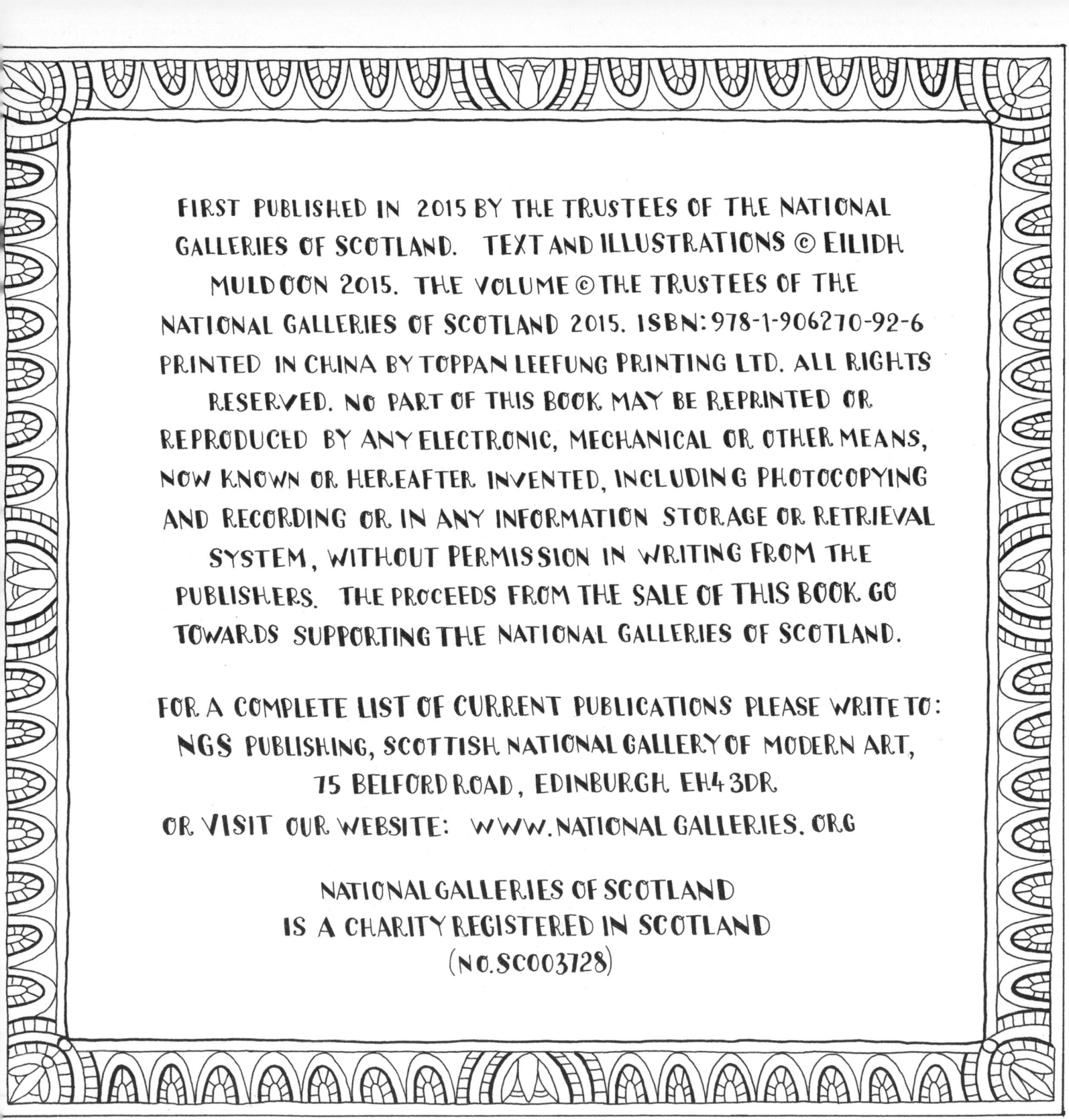

FIRST PUBLISHED IN 2015 BY THE TRUSTEES OF THE NATIONAL GALLERIES OF SCOTLAND. TEXT AND ILLUSTRATIONS © EILIDH MULDOON 2015. THE VOLUME © THE TRUSTEES OF THE NATIONAL GALLERIES OF SCOTLAND 2015. ISBN: 978-1-906270-92-6 PRINTED IN CHINA BY TOPPAN LEEFUNG PRINTING LTD. ALL RIGHTS RESERVED. NO PART OF THIS BOOK MAY BE REPRINTED OR REPRODUCED BY ANY ELECTRONIC, MECHANICAL OR OTHER MEANS, NOW KNOWN OR HEREAFTER INVENTED, INCLUDING PHOTOCOPYING AND RECORDING OR IN ANY INFORMATION STORAGE OR RETRIEVAL SYSTEM, WITHOUT PERMISSION IN WRITING FROM THE PUBLISHERS. THE PROCEEDS FROM THE SALE OF THIS BOOK GO TOWARDS SUPPORTING THE NATIONAL GALLERIES OF SCOTLAND.

FOR A COMPLETE LIST OF CURRENT PUBLICATIONS PLEASE WRITE TO:
NGS PUBLISHING, SCOTTISH NATIONAL GALLERY OF MODERN ART,
75 BELFORD ROAD, EDINBURGH EH4 3DR
OR VISIT OUR WEBSITE: WWW.NATIONALGALLERIES.ORG

NATIONAL GALLERIES OF SCOTLAND
IS A CHARITY REGISTERED IN SCOTLAND
(NO. SC003728)